THE AGISTER'S EXPERIMENT

by Gill Learner

To Megs (who remembers my life better than I do!) with lots of love

Gill x

First published in the UK in 2010 by

Two Rivers Press
35–39 London Street
Reading RG1 4PS
www.tworiverspress.com

Two Rivers Press is represented in the UK by Inpress Ltd.
and distributed by Central Books

Cover design: Sally Castle
Text design: Nadja Guggi

Printed and bound by Imprint Digital, Exeter

Copyright © Gill Learner 2010

The right of Gill Learner to be identified as the author of this work has been asserted by her in accordance with the Copyright, Designs and Patents Act of 1988

ISBN 978-1-901677-71-3

Acknowledgements

I am very grateful to Susan Utting and members of
her classes for inspiration and feedback, to my fellow poets
in Thin Raft poetry workshops, to Helena Nelson
of Happen*stance* for her encouragement and, particularly,
to Jane Draycott for her invaluable comments on
the manuscript.

My thanks also to the editors of the following where
versions of some of these poems have appeared:
magazines *14*, *Aesthetica Creative Works Annual 2009*,
Artemis, *Envoi*, *Poetry Ealing*, *Poetry Life*, *Poetry News*,
Smiths Knoll, *South*, *Sphinx*, *Tears in the Fence*, *The French
Literary Review*, *The Interpreter's House*, *The Unruly Sun*;
Manchester Cathedral Prize pamphlet 2008; anthologies
My Mother Threw Knives (Second Light Publications),
Hand Luggage Only (Open Poetry), *Outbox* (Leaf Books),
Petra Kenney Prize pamphlet 2006, *The River Thames
in Verse* (River Thames Society), *The Ticking Crocodile*
(Blinking Eye), *A Twist of Malice* and *Cracking On*
(Grey Hen Press), *Seeking Refuge* (Cinnamon Press);
www.readinglibraries.org.uk, www.writersbureau.com,
www.marplewriting.org.uk and www.bbc.co.uk/radio3/
classical/tchaikovsky/competition.

'About the olden days' was first published in *Poetry News*
and was awarded the Poetry Society's Hamish Canham
Prize 2008.

Note
*Agisters are officials in the New Forest and are responsible
for overseeing all aspects of the livestock roaming there.*

*In memory of my parents,
Guy and Jay Lovekin*

Contents

The craft | 13
The agister's experiment | 14
Element 84 | 15
Country church | 16
Make-ready | 17
Banged out | 18
About the olden days | 19
Tough love | 20
Witch | 22
A matter of superstition | 23
Brought up by hand | 24
Da capo | 25
Trying it on | 26
Exile | 28
Counted out | 29
My father sees red | 30
Carmelites | 31
Belonging | 32
A sense of the river | 34
From grilse to kelt | 35
Mapped/unmapped | 36
Rain, steam and speed | 37
Clogs | 38
Painted from life | 39
Through and through | 40
Ashok dreaming | 41
More than words | 42
The certainty of bats | 44
Future simple | 45

The descent from Mount Olympus | 46
Larder | 47
Becoming | 48
Without the hat | 49
Advice to new owners | 50
Not for sale | 51
Beginning notes | 52
Piano man | 53
Epitaph for George Russell | 54
The search for perfection | 56
Comprehension test | 57
Foot down | 58
The calorific value of anxiety | 59
Fahrenheit 451 | 60
How to build a cathedral | 61
Quartet for the end of time | 62

Time

It will pass, it can heal, it may fly;
ours to stall for, or play for, or buy.
We can save, serve or fill it;
waste, mark, call or kill it.
But it's up at the moment we die.

The craft
for Jez and Jen

As for a boat he worked the wood:
curving it wide at the shoulders
by cutting the internal ply, the two-by-one struts,
narrowing down to the foot.
It was measured and made for a friend.

Unvarnished it hung some years in the barn
with a glossy canoe –
a Shire stabled next to an Arab –
without brasses, not meant for show or endurance,
a simple container.

Death arrived. Not for the man who bespoke it
but for the carpenter's mother.
It was manhandled into the Astra,
ferried across the Cambrian mountains, the Severn
and down to the Solent.

Padded with straw
and New Forest beech leaves
under a sheet of drawn-threadwork,
it was set up on trestles, lid off for looking or chatting
in lavender-rosemary air.

A gentian-blue cover was scattered
with primroses, iris, an apple-flower wreath.
Four women lifted and steadied it, strode with it;
carried their grandma,
not to the sea but the fire.

The agister's experiment

At last the time had come – both animals were
sparking on all cylinders. My moon-white Isis
was as twitchy as a loose-end flex, silk-purse ears
pointing then flattening – half readiness,
half fear. She heard his protest, felt threat
and promise in the thud of hooves on wood,
swivelled her eyes, jerked the tether, sent tremors
rippling from mane to tail.

He was a rumour stalked for years
through brambles, nettles. Dung-rubbed,
I crouched in bracken, watched him graze
among oaks and beeches like a ghost of himself;
his antler tapered almost straight from his broad
pale forehead. Him I'd arrowed quiet, pulled
from the forest, stalled and fed to hard fitness.
I opened the door on her.

It didn't take long. At first she balked, strained
at the hobbles, then steadied, tail held aside.
As fear was conquered by his drive, I clipped one ear
with a device by which to track him if this trial fails.
Two months I nannied her until I knew she'd held;
a further eight of cosseting. One day very soon
I'll know if it must be done again, or if at last
I've bred a unicorn.

Element 84

Last autumn I discovered
pentacles inked on paving
by fallen plane-tree leaves.
But they brought to mind
shadows photo'd onto stone
by an intensity of light.

If she'd known maybe she'd have
pushed that unremitting energy
back into the box before
the laying waste to bones
that could have set a counter
chattering like frenzied castanets.

Then that firefly glow might not
have grown into a thousand suns
that roared like Zeus's fury
on two August days. But
shrapnel and bullets would have
festered undetected, damage
to shattered limbs remained
a guess; tumours gnawed
further into organs, flesh.

My ghost-leaves will be
gone by the time
the daffodils appear.

Country church

Beyond the argument of rooks, the scratch
of yews, tick of gravestones leaning a further
thousandth of an inch, I catch the phantom creak
of wheels along the old straight track. Propped
by rough-cut granite, my shoulders tingle
to the dot-year chip and scrape of chisels,
mortar-slap, levelling knock of trowels.

Through the fissured history of the door
I skirt memorial slabs, by grudging light
make out a martyr's fate in faded browns
and blues on plaster blotched with damp.
Should I take heed of warnings in the frieze:
hell-flames licking, demons swallowing?
I recognise mischief in one corbel's grin, malice
in another's; wonder who the masons meant.

Barrel vaulting has absorbed the shrill
and drone of hymns through a millennium.
The nave holds echoes of vows exchanged,
baptismal cries and smothered grief. If
there were candles, I would light one
to enjoy a glow warming the altar stone,
watch shadows scrabbling the walls,
smell the warmth of bees.

At the door again, I post a coin into
the wall-set box, turn and see the font.
What I took for leafy ornament now
shows a face, branches spreading
from between its teeth. Was he cut
to placate the ancient gods? In a sudden
flush of sun, one eye seems to blink.

Make-ready

This he believes – that in this secret plying of his craft
he formulates a prayer for equal rights
for all his fellow men to work and earn and eat.
He knows that if he's caught indentures will be forfeited,
his father's payments thrown away, his mother's heart
in pieces like a window smashed.

Of this he's sure: where each letter waits. He chooses,
feels for the nick, clicks it into place until
the stick is filled. Two blocks of lines from ore
hacked free, melted then solidified. He locks and inks,
pulls proofs, scans and corrects
what few can read but all may sing.

The forme disguised, the stone re-shone, he feels
a kick of fear in the tired street. He runs
with a jolt on his thigh of the pasteboard
black with the Frenchman's song which swells
in his head so he dares shout the comrade world awake
to rise, unite and face the final fight.

Banged out

Some days his right hand forgets its cunning. Although
it knows the case like Ellie's body, suddenly it muddles
p and *q*, fails to lock up tight, ends with pie.

Between times he could weep at newspapers with titling
not kerned or letterspaced, *f* and *i* unligatured, flyers
home-composed in a mishmash of typefaces.

Some days his feet forget the way. He fumbles
his key into a long-ago lock, snarls at the new owner,
at Ellie arriving to steer him home.

Usually, though, he changes his shoes as soon
as he gets in, asks how she's been, washes up without
a chip, remembers the grandchildren's names.

Today, even after several in the pub, he walks straight
and tall through the crash of chases and galleys,
the cheers of comps who didn't serve

their seven years, wouldn't know an em quad
from a quoin, depend on algorithms to split words.
He's the last of the hot metal men.

But today is a fine day.

About the olden days

Tell me how water magnified the surfaces of leaves
or skittered off. How it spilled from tiles, gargled
along gutters, dropped into echoing butts.
How earth absorbed and hoarded it in lightless caves,
returned it at springs where women left offerings.

Talk about cumulus, cirrus, stratus,
and watching thunderheads approach. How light
thickened from gold to green, how water felt
slipping down cheeks to dusty lips. About cycling
in a yellow oilskin tent, head bent against the sting.

Describe brollies, wellies, puddles and the smell
of dampened soil. How you would hunt for newts,
pick meadow-sweet, try to spot sundew trapping flies.
Explain drizzle, scattered showers, cats-and-dogs.
Please, before we burn, tell me about rain.

Tough love

They were desperate times. For months dust devils danced
across the plain. Our river's great skeins dwindled to
a thread; pomegranates shrivelled. Tempers ran short:
men fought in the market-place, filched from neighbours' fields.
Then, one fiery afternoon a voice vibrated
in my head, giving me instructions strange but clear.

The day our boat was roofed, my Hannah smelled water
on the wind. Our deck was not yet caulked when cloud boiled
from the north. Thunder raised lions' hackles, scattered
goats and sheep. When the first drops pocked the sand, Hannah
slapped the horses forward and ran to heave a sack
of almonds in by jars of honey, vats of oil –

for a voyage God knew where, for how many days …
or years. Dry springs leapt alive, spilled into hollows
which filled and met, were swallowed by the river as
it welled and spread. The vessel lurched so that we slid,
righted, began to swing. Plugging our ears to pleas
we raised the sail, started to skim above the palms.

I love my kindred but to be confined with them
spins patience to a wire. The three boys disputed
who should muck out and who keep watch; their wives
      complained
of the damp, the diet of nuts and cold dried fruit –
our bread had grown mould, we couldn't cook grain or roots
for we did not dare a fire. Hannah groomed rabbits

bred to feed carnivores, faked confidence in me
but when she thought me out of hearing, prayed for help
to Lady Asherah of the Sea. Each took time
at some hour of the day to pause and gaze across
the endless folding-over of the waves to where
sky and water blurred in shafts of unceasing rain.

At last, with food and forage low, the battering
on the roof grew fainter, stopped. We clambered on deck,
raked the rim of our world for bumps. I went below,
brought up a raven, tossed it to the clouds. Three days
we watched in vain. So I released a dove but she
was crooning on the roof before the light had gone.

Sleep was now a treacherous friend: the creatures howled;
our bellies growled in sympathy. After a week,
hope withering, I launched the dove again. As night
turned thick I saw her wings flicker against the moon,
coaxed her down with corn; she let fall an olive-twig
on my foot. My laughter hauled them stumbling from bed.

God's breath nudged us to a mountainside. I slaughtered
our first calf, set it on fire as thanks; the fragrance
brought moisture to our mouths. God said we could now
eat flesh, killed clean. We were commissioned, man and beast,
to disperse and breed, for never again would earth
be cursed by him. The pledge's sign rose from the waves,

over our tilted heads and down, in half a hoop
of seven blending shades. It's to be thus: we'll have
moonlight and sun in turn, planting and gathering,
warmth and chill, with mastery over all that breathe
and swim. But we must never shed a fellow's blood.
God knows that man's a fool yet trusts him with the world.

Witch

Mine is the skill to straddle a ragwort stalk,
rise against the moon, stir the stars and skim
the chimneys prodding the sky at the end
of the land, or shift my shape to owl or hare
and arc across the moor.

Mine is the craft bought with the midnight touch,
nine-times, of the logan stone, and in church
with wine, the wafer saved to feed a toad,
and three times said 'Our father', end to start,
to woo the outside gods.

Mine are the charms to summon sudden storms
when rich ships ride the tide, shine lights
to warn of thrashing seas, bounce balls of fire
up carns or down the shafts and tunnels
lined with copper veins.

Mine is the gift to sail in a bladebone boat,
call down the wind or sell it to sailors: knots
on a thread to be unstrung, one for a breath,
two for a gale behind, three to blow
the vessel safely home.

Yours is the power to steal my strength
with an onion stuck with pins to pain my limbs,
a waxen manikin thrown into the flames,
a silver bullet, a shovelful of fire …
if you should dare.

A matter of superstition

This is a mouse which might have been
the soul of an average man,
laid careful schemes, been given a fright
beneath a throne, or sung a rhythmic tune
of notes as high and thin as wire.

This is a mouse which might have lived off
candles in a crypt, nibbled at clothes
and brought bad luck, been asked politely
please to go elsewhere, set free a lion
caught in a net (though probably not round here).

This is a mouse not boiled or fried and
mixed with jam as a cure for whooping cough,
or chased by an angry farmer's wife,
or nimble enough to evade our cat
who caught and killed it,
brought it in,
ate all but the head
on which I trod
                              barefoot.

Brought up by hand

My grandmother is playing her book. Her eyes are fixed
on an invisible horizon of marshland, a churchyard,
hulks slumped at anchor. As her foxed hands slide
from side to side, her wedding ring winks useless light.
The flesh beneath her nails is bleached and the pale tips
of keratin are as thin as threads. The polished pads
have whorls worn faint and overscored with creases
mapping four-fifths of a century. She strokes words
off the page then gives them to the air in a hesitant
incantation I can hardly hear: *forge, Pip, Joe Gargery*.
Each letter, dash and comma is recorded there,
in a matrix of six dots embossed on weighty paper.
Once I loved her fingers' creep across my face but now
allow only a graze of flesh on flesh in case she reads
the lies, dodged fares, the fifty-penny pieces filched
from my mother's purse, the unconfessed carpark nudge,
the drunken shag with the nameless man from Leeds.

Da capo

Sing it all: from rock-a-bye to rock around the clock
by way of rushes-o and foggy dew.

Once I stood on Basin Street, drank lilac wine,
thought foolish things about my careless love.

Even when I'd moved to grown-up stuff – malo malo malo;
Requiem aeternam in half a dozen settings –
I'd let the willow, willow weep for me.

Favourites come and go – new almost every morning
but rarely hymns, though sheep may safely graze,
and a winter journey lifts the soul if I can steal away.

Most words are lost but melodies bounce on between the ears,
insistent as the phone that rings but who's to answer.

As time goes by it nudges me toward the unknown region
with its California dreams and no regrets.

Trying it on

The razzle-dazzle trawls us in, Janet and me,
we are netted by noise – the pound of generators,
hurdy-gurdy giddy music. Deep breaths of hurrying
capture fried onions, engine fumes, spun sugar.

Queuing, sixpences clutched, we watch the bikers
park Ariels and Beezers with a backward jerk,
shake down their drainpipes for a crêpe-soled strut.
We look away, turning up our collars and our noses.

Hand-painted light-bulbs, blobbed and scratched,
fight with summer evening sun, illuminating stalls
piled-high with cut-glass vases, plaster figurines,
teddy bears, and lollipops as consolation prizes.

The Big Wheel turns its slow, chair-lurching circle
and from the top we see houses, pubs and shops
lined up to head for Stratford, point out the Odeon,
the junior school I left four years ago.

Dodgems shake our teeth as, obeying the injunction
not to crash, we're bashed by boys pretending innocence.
The Wall of Death whirls, pressing our bodies outwards till,
once we are pinned in gravity-defiance, the floor recedes.

Two lads we know are trailing us, nudging and daring.
They take us on the Waltzer where, wild and dizzy
in its double gyre, we scream in simulated fear
and feel their soft arms tighten round our shoulders.

They test their skills on sideshows, but targets
they pock with shot stay upright, cards they spear
with darts score only enough for sweets, and
coconuts won't fall. Janet is better at them all.

In the Ghost Train's cobwebbed semi-darkness
we giggle at goblins, ghosts and witches,
submit to tickly, bum-fluff kisses, but allow
no liberties or anything that messes up our hair.

Outside, the boys light up Park Drives, cupped
in apprentice palms, and offer us a second ride.
But it's nearly half-past nine; we hurry off
with no intriguing footwear left behind.

That night I dream of vortices and flight
and speeding to Stratford on the pillion of a bike.

Exile
For Bruce

He left behind the red-brick villas, gravel beds
and lakes of sand spread with the river's flood.

In a land of gritstone walls where flat is rare,
an alien among worshippers of different gods,
he drills his children in the canticles of home.
Before they're old enough to understand,
even less attend the ceremonials,
they can recite the sacred calls,
cheer with same-faith bands who pilgrim north.

At play these infant acolytes rehearse the adult rituals
with a model of the talisman, at an altar improvised
from bricks against the fence. Robed in red, they lift
their shining voices in defiant conjurations:
van Persie, Walcott, Fabregas.

Counted out
In memory of Grandad Harold 1884–1972

It was quite a jump from Highbury to Amiens,
from hefting sides of pork to stacking the cart
with crates of bully beef, barbed wire,
steadying the nag when thunder
crumped too near, crooning what came easy
to an ostler's son but couldn't always
still the flinch of hide; and no good to grow
too fond of a handy screen.
                           It was a far cry
from feathers, Maud's rump in his lap
and Little Connie's dreams a reach away,
to a doss-down in a blackened barn,
the shift of hooves in the splintered night,
trying to block out yells by reliving bouts
at Clifton Star A.C., struggling to recall
the brine-smell as they trundled in the chara
to Southend.
               It was a long, long way, chlorine
fizzing in his lungs – caught before he'd time
to tie a piss-soaked handkerchief over his face –
to the scurry of nurses, soothe of milk,
and the cough that never frightened off
the ten a day of Craven A until
it all went quiet.

My father sees red

It was second-hand, The Sunbeam,
fifty bob. Ten years old but tank still black,
gold leaf mostly good. First motorbike.

As he revved away, a Curragh breath
ghosted in his ear *Remember, Master Guy:
head up, heels down, back straight.*
Suddenly he's eight and in suspense, thighs
tight to Spartan's saddle, dodging mounts as jittery
as the men looming at Father's factory gate.

A horn cuts through the frost to a counterpoint
of hounds speaking to the scent. Mustn't
let Ryan down *Elbows in, toes front.*

The chase is glorious – specs wedged
under his cap, full gallop after scarlet coats;
he and the pony wing over every hedge.
At the kill he looks away but there's no escape –
the MFH comes at him with the brush. He gulps
at the stickiness on his cheeks, the reek of fox.

He propped the Sunbeam by the paper shop,
came out with his usual – ten Woodbines
and the *Daily Worker* tucked inside his coat.

Carmelites

The cloistered aristos don't stand a chance
against the *sans-culottes*. The clunk
of Poulenc's guillotine whittles at the chorus
so that *Salve Regina* becomes thinner and
thinner until the last voice is stopped.

*

My mother's six. Wide-eyed at so many
Sacred Hearts and yet not Church, she's left
'just for the afternoon'. While, in a squeal
of slates she sits with aproned girls, a little case
is slipped upstairs. At supper, trying to swallow,
aware of the silent skim of habits, she's waiting
for the smiling one to say 'Come, Joyce, you're
going home'. Later a room with twenty beds,
the folded vests she searches through for
some loved thing, finds only a rosary
she hardly knows how to use.

                                                Six months
with no familiar face. Some letters from sisters –
Ilma about munitions work, Marie nursing
shell-shocked boys, both walking out with this
young man or that. Best, from brother Tom, folded
round a shore-leave photograph – he's grinning
behind his pipe, crowded by four other tars,
H.M.S. Excellence askew above their eyes –
with a promise that next time he docks
he'll fetch her home.

*

After the trouserless, only a church still stands –
for Saint Symphorien who also lost his head
though over Cybele. By its walls, where monks
once scuffed their naked soles, *les enfants
d'Avignon* squeal down a scarlet slide,
bounce on sprung animals.

Belonging

Best forget the dream: a gilded day with sugared grass,
breath fluffed round our heads; a crystal glide
from underground to scatter light before we clouded it
with Grandad's dust. The infant stream had sprawled,
hidden its birth in lakes which once were fields.
The river writes the rules.

At least the wind was with us, pushing its breath
along the flow. It wafted floury particles but let grit drop
like winnowed grain from the parapet of Ha'penny Bridge.
For a second, ashes scummed the swell that
simmered east then clotted, swirled, went down
as the river received its own.

He was a Millwall man, whose living Devlin did for,
last in a line of stevedores and lightermen
with muscles like mooring ropes, hands of seasoned teak,
who'd seen water stained with indigo, coal, blood;
and women who'd scrubbed shirts which smelled of lemons,
cinnamon, tea, tobacco, or sewage after a fall:
the river's not always cruel.

Let those crumbs carry in the drift to where brine begins
then sink and settle, add to silt on stones he skimmed,
fragments of letter-freighting bottles, pins that fastened
matchwood rafts he saw propeller-churned to splinters.
From eighty years ago when the moon governed these games,
the river ran through his dreams.

He turned a bitter back as cranes swung over building sites
and the rattle of anchor chains gave way to shouted deals
from would-be Whittingtons. As houses grew where cows
    once grazed
so that Kennet, Colne and Wey were forced downstream,
and winter water spilled and spread back across ancient plains,
he shook his head: *Will they never learn?*
The river always wins.

A sense of the river

Here is a congregation of empty fingers,
gathered together over years: blue
as the Piccadilly line, vivid as Arsenal strip,
creamy as St Paul's. These didn't

snug the hands of surgeons or beauticians
but their touch could be as delicate – tickling
the hulls of refuse barges, disco boats;
soothing pier supports and steps. They stroked

the limbs of washed-up Barbie dolls,
fumbled in burger boxes, frisked oyster shells
for pearls. They arpeggio'd on bike wheels,
jingled the xylophone of roof-tiles jostling

on a beach, castenetted broken plates.
Pock-marked by chemicals, blistered by oil,
they survived the pricks and tourniquets
of hook and line. But without the puppetry

of tides or hands kept safe while hefting
breeze-blocks, laying tarmac, trimming joists,
they're lifeless, subverted into art. Now
there's only thumbs up or a V-sign at the past.

Michael O'Reilly collected objects from beside the Thames and grouped them by type for an exhibition of photographs: 'Fragments from the foreshore'

From grilse to kelt

The undark of the ward snuffles round my bed.
I lie weightless, exhausted but taut
with elation, adrift on anglers' lore:

how a fierce tide prickles in the gathered fat,
urges the salmon from rich feeding towards
one-way water; how she aims her snub

at the bland flow which tries to redirect
the motor-force pushing her on. Skin tarnishing,
she dodges night nets, growling knives, circles

below a weir to find the deepest scoop,
builds speed for the muscle-clench projection.
She rises with the temperature, reversing the run

of fork-tailed fingerling to find the gravel nest
she struggled from. Into a new hollow
her wasted body gives up its amber beads.

Emptied, we slide together in the slow descent;
let the downstream carry us towards the sea.

Mapped/Unmapped

Look at these black filaments: they pull us along them,
straight as engineers could build, sliced through rock, stilted
over valleys. They hide between rabbit-riddled banks
      of buddleia
and willowherb, or travel high on gritty ridges slunk by foxes.

Now run your fingers down these heavy cables, blue
in sight and sign, that spider out from the metropolis,
      or unroll
uninterrupted north to south, their sapling-skewered verges
the habitat of scurrying creatures, overhung with kestrels.

Red ropes are purposeful: laid out for soldiers' marching,
for wagons of wool or corn, for carriages and coaches. Factories
now escort them to where shops give way to villas, magpied
playing fields, then acres of oil-seed rape and sheep.

See these? Yellow yarn that curls along ancient tracks:
the easy-walking ways from settlement to village, farm
      to market.
Goosegrass and bramble cushion their banks, hawthorn
      and holly
screen them, brilliant with boasts of wrens and robins.

Best are the ligatures that stutter their green dots away from
office blocks, across unfolding spaces. They lead us to
threads of blue, uncertain as unpicked knitting, scoured
through lows, ghostly with trout, flashed by kingfishers.

And last there are the wires – invisible, taut as nerves –
that stretch from tumulus to holy well, from church to
      hill-fort,
sarsen to sacred grove, tying the land and charged
with energies man can no longer understand.

Rain, steam and speed
by J.M.W. Turner

Look how, against a weight of strange beliefs,
the hare lopes from beam to beam
between the singing bars then hears above
a harrow's scrape and dancers' calls,
the growl of some strange creature larger
than a horse, deadlier than the blades that shred
his field in shrinking rings; hears the growl
become a roar and, scalloping the air,
stretches to escape the iron and smoke,
westward through dissolving sun and storm.

Poor hare, that in this new millennium
cannot outrun the train.

Clogs
by Vincent van Gogh, Arles 1888

They're sturdy, this pair of pattens, defiant
in their own shadow on a bench. Thick uppers

look unyielding yet feet have sculpted them
to plantar arch, twisted toe and bunion.

A single block made sole and heel: prow-lift fore,
raised platform aft. No sign of studs or pins –

a rim of hidden nails must fasten hide to wood.
Age has worn both materials to drab,

reproduced in chisel-stripes blunt with haste
or passion. These sabots are seasoned but

not trodden down; fissured where weather's
bled the skin. Perhaps the cracks store

market dregs or midden ooze that spice
the smell of seasoned saddlery.

Do they dance, nights, to a secret orchestra
of Catherine-wheeling stars?

Maybe they'd fit me. When I slide them on
I'll find them ghostly warm, but alien.

Painted from life

Bored with his skin, the Impressionist winds
a chrome green stalk from toe to crutch
of his left leg, adds viridian leaves,
lets sweet peas coil in purple and cochineal.
He draws the other leg to life
with nasturtium vines: emerald foliage,
cornets of Naples yellow and vermilion.
For his back he needs a looking glass,
long brushes: foxglove and larkspur leap –
rose madder and cerulean – from a shrubbery
of verditer and jade. Chest and belly bloom
with dahlias in Indian yellow, cinnabar
and Lemnian earth. One arm grows violas
all mauve and orpiment, the other borage
in cobalt bleached with lead white.
Ferns creep from his beard to curl
across his brow in shades of Scheele's green.

Wound in a cloak he walks to the park
and unwraps his latest work.
Children stop bowling hoops to stare,
ladies' eyes widen behind their veils,
gentlemen shout *Shame*. He laughs and runs.

Although the canvas slackens, he fights
to keep the flowers bright,
but now the brush feels weighted,
dithers in his grip.
Under the dahlias his innards twist.

The men shrug at the colours,
blurred and bleeding one into another,
as they furl him in his shroud.

Through and through

I never tired of watching him at work, itching
to collect the forbidden litter of his craft – glittery
like the remnants of a crown. Before the war
he sketched a promise of my own, with dragonflies
and reeds, but a mortar in the fight for Anzio
stilled the welted hands that had refused to hold a gun,
chose stretcher-poles instead.

Years on, stepping from lake to coloured lake
in Notre-Dame of Chartres, I feel my nape-hair rise
at the shades of *maîtres verriers* eight centuries gone
who placed alongside saints their fellow artisans:
wheelwright, cooper and apothecary, a wine-grower
treading grapes. My father would have honoured
the artists' genius if not their god.

The remembered fumes of solder sear my nose,
I hear the scrit of a scoring tool, the crunch and snap
as crescents, triangles, and random shapes
are bitten from sheets of glass: heaven in speedwell blue,
haloes the red of sun on my closed eyes,
robes like bluebell leaves, the gold of marmalade for
      angels' hair;
lead strips to rim and bind.

He could never cycle past a church but must go in,
examine another's work, critique, admire, till my mother
led me into the air for our necks to straighten among
      the stones.
A glazier, he'd say, *fills holes for light, and sight
onto the world, while I make images to linger on.*
By focussing its power through chromatic chemistry,
he dared manipulate the sun.

Ashok dreaming

No more school. He writes only in his head while
fishing fuzzy eggs from killing vats. He thinks
on paper white as yarn from worms fed
finest mulberry, smooth as the scarless skin
inside his upper arm. Even with a pen, he couldn't
form the loops and curls like patterns drawn by
women's dancing hands – his fingers ache and burn.

No school now. Steamy days fumble into night.
While he flicks out boiled cocoons, he lives again
his sister's wedding days: flocks of saris – mango,
pomegranate, lime – with golden edgings winking
at the sun. With noontime rice he tastes
the feast again: crunch of puri, chili fire, spice
of halva, kulfi sweet and icy on his tongue.

Six days a week he's winding to machines.
But the man who bought him doesn't often beat,
sells food cheap, gives paste for healing wounds.
Once the dowry debt is paid, he'll go back to school,
make sense of chalk-marks, count beyond his fingers.
He'll become a doctor, take a wife, dress her
in silk that's spun and woven by free hands.

More than words

*Women of Hunan province have, since at least
the beginning of the Qing dynasty (1644–1912),
used a phonetic writing system known only
to themselves*

1.
So she conjures Nushu for her sworn sisters,
turns a cane in the soot of a cooking-pot,
codes endurance on a handkerchief
in elongated arcs, squeezed crosses, forks.
She draws the sting of her husband's
mother's tongue, the breathless sweat of night.

Characters trickle down the woven page,
and down again, patterning the white
with separation, the icy slap
of river washing, squint of tiny stitches,
slice of running cotton as it reels and reels.

She mouths the comfort-sounds
of the woman-script her mother taught
while brothers sat in school, feels the crush
of strap-cloths on her infant feet,
the stutter over village cobbles, hums

then sings out loud the sister-songs.

2.
It should have passed with her into the light,
my grandmother's Third-day Book, to be read
by ancestral eyes. But it was kept back, hidden
like imperial jade. From it my child-tongue
traced the falling flowers of Nushu syllables,
stumbled through motherly instructions
to be virtuous and obedient, indulgent
with sons, diligent over daughters.

From my aunt's I stroked soft curves,
her hand guiding mine on the brush. While
my brothers learned broad-shouldered words,
I copied the sorrow of her sworn sisters
at the coming distance, pledges that love
would tie them across river and mountain.
I patterned without understanding
invasion, violation, shame.

Yesterday my girl was a three-day bride.
Two pages of her red-bound book deliver
my tender wishes, advice that she love her man
but let him know her strength. Next,
her friends define their parting grief, swear
a walk of half a day won't part them long.
Soon her pen will unroll its secrets
down the waiting leaves.

The certainty of bats

It's this pale evening
on which bats draw
Pythagorean diagrams,
rulering from the indigo
of the walnut tree,
out of sight beyond the gable,
back, wiping speckles
from the dusk.
                      The sky loiters,
pulled towards midnight
but not ready to let go.
Bleached, it is waiting
for the sun's absence
to ink it in
           and this is how
we find our selves, suspended
between hoping and knowing,
between what should have been
and what is.

Future simple

Tomorrow
I will smile
and later
I'll unlock
my tongue
so *Thankyou*
can spring out.
A week from now
I'll haul my costume on,
slide into the pool and glide,
arms and legs in rhythmic flex and flow.
Next, I'll sip from a china cup, not spill a drop.
Within two weeks I'll push against the arms, rise
leaning slightly on the frame, extend one foot then
overtake it with its mate – ten times to cross the room.
Before six months is up, I'll walk to the shop with sticks,
wave at a bus, deal silver from my purse and pick up
change.
After a rest,
I'll do buttons.

The descent from Mount Olympus

Where to begin? Maybe after the centuries
in earth, your power leaking into dark, when
a rough-palmed farmer knocked his plough
against your neck, hauled you to heat
and scent of dittany. Bargained over, saved
from the Turks, crated, cranked aboard without
due care so that you broke in half and lost
two limbs which ghost-ache in the northern chill.

Or start perhaps with the man from Antioch
unlocking you from rock, chip by considered
chip, until you stood, torso twisted, right hand
offering a pomegranate, draped sacrum to foot
in rigid folds with belly, breasts and shoulders
bare to Anatolian air.

No. Let's begin in the time of cherishing, high
on a hill, in a citadel where white doves picked
at votive corn, then crooned in sweet-oiled myrtles;
where you received the prayers of those
who sought to find or keep true love, and
offerings of women longing for a child. Was it
Hephaistos' rage or Athens' battering rams
that crushed your shrine to brash?

So, all the beginnings are told. Now there's
no chime of orioles or crush of thyme beneath
the feet of acolytes and only a cleaner's cloth
to tease from throat to waist, draw spirals round
your navel. Never the touch of loving hands.
This is how it ends.

Larder

In case this harvest doesn't last, I'll set something by:
fire a drum of applewood to smoke split kisses;
fillet laughter, pack it into pots with oil and herbs.
I'll seal your voice in shiny tins, string private jokes
and dry them, press a bunch of your best anecdotes.

Your hangovers will enrich the compost heap, along
with whinges when I come home late, flu-induced
self-pity, a taste for horror films. And I'll throw on
football absences and Leonard Cohen times.

But against the day the cornucopia runs out,
I'll have a hoard: memories of Norway layered in salt;
whispers distilled in tiny bottles; vacuum-packs
of secret looks; nights simmered in honeydew, poured
into jars and stored where the sun shines through.

Becoming
for Eva

Daddy calls you Princess and you're longing
for the whole pink-satin-bodices-with-bows,
stardust Disney thing,
with of course the handsome prince,
who'll have more hair than Daddy,
and a horse.

But think ...
do you want to end up slung across a saddle
never handling the reins yourself,
or clean and cook for seven little men
then be poisoned with an apple?
Could you bear to be abducted
by a dragon?

Would you wish to wed a man
more simple than his cat;
to be a pawn in bargainings with Beasts
or diminutive-but-cunning tailors?
Could you let a wily servant trick you into
minding geese?

Imagine hospitality
involving twenty mattresses piled above a pea,
or dancing secretly
while a smart-arse soldier spies on you.
And let's not even think
about the frog.

So aim to skipper England's football squad,
conduct the last night of the Proms, direct the BBC.
And can we hope
one day to see a woman
Primate of all England
or even Pope?

Without the hat
for Pam

It used to be his party trick, she said,
over a five-barred gate. One minute
we'd be looking at the view,
the next he'd spring into the air,
appear to pause in his lateral glide
then drop down on the other side.
Or when things were quiet at work,
they'd clear the top of a plan chest
and, from standing still, he'd make
a vertical ascent then land with a soft thud
and a creak from the surprised wood;
they'd all applaud.

I picture him – dark and slight,
suited and tied, theodolite in hand –
elevate on tiny pin-striped wings.
He hangs beneath the neon lights,
over the blueprint-sheeted desks,
the slide-rules and pots of pens,
like a figure from Magritte
without the bowler hat.

Of course, she said, he had to stop
after his heart attack.

Advice to new owners

The item you have just acquired requires care.
Do not expose to sunlight, guard from frost.

Violent agitation can harm delicate components
but if disturbance does occur give time for settling.

Alcohol should be avoided before and during contact.
Smoking is not advised. Keep away from naked flame.

As each article is custom-made,
there will be variations in pigment and design.

Regular cleaning will prevent discolouration –
handwash in warm water, do not drip-dry.

Although you'll find it flexible and water-tolerant,
prolonged immersion will prove damaging.

Irritation may occur – if this becomes excessive
seek professional advice.

By taking this delivery you agree to these conditions.
You have no statutory rights, only obligations.

It is hoped your baby brings you lots of joy.

Not for sale

No-one can buy me. I'm mercury and if you try to grab me
I'll dribble from your clutch. My song is like the humming
of the stars, or the hush in seashells. I can melt your brain into
hallucination, or tease you like a name you can't recall.

There's no bargaining: I dole out favours on a whim. In dim-
lit theatres I may hold you for a while then let you drop so that
you jump. I can touch your mouth with honey but usually
I coat your tongue with dust of ancient libraries.

I don't have a price. If you think you can seduce me
with excessive wine, I'll humour you then
leave abruptly only to return just prior to the jeers
of the alarm. And my grit will fill your eyes for hours.

If I wish to I may drown you in my dolphin deep,
keep you there or swoop you to the surface, immerse
and wash you up repeatedly until you weep for peace.
No-one can buy me. I'm remedy, renewal; I am …

                                                        shhhh.

Beginning notes
after Walt Whitman

'Out of the cradle endlessly rocking' flows down the page –
      a barefoot boyhood remembered –
and I am ten again and with my father listening to *Sea drift*
      on the wireless,
a she-child, knowing only Blyton and Streatfeild,
but feeling in the grey-blue Delius chords, in the shadowy
      baritone words,
above all in my father's telling of the unnamed bird calling,
      calling for his mate,
the sadness of unexplained loss.

The only love I knew was for my parents,
the only sorrow for my cat found dead at the side of the road,
but I was lifted from the fireside and set down
      on the only shore I knew,
a shingle beach where Cader Idris starts its slow climb
      out of Merioneth surf,
where I now became either he-child or bird, sending
      a gentle call out across the waves
for future lovers who might not return.

And more than ever as the sea 'whisper'd me',
the boy's pain, the bird's pain, perhaps my father's pain,
      became mine.

Piano man
In April 2005 a young man was found wandering on a beach in Kent.

He planned it well –
another country,
labels clipped from clothes, rubbed from shoes.

But even the sea rejected him.

He was found; clothed, fed, and given
music:
his tongue was numb but his hands spoke.

Maybe the sea had taken something after all –
an awkwardness of muscle, unwillingness
of ligament, inability of metacarpal
to move to the brain's waves;
twenty years' anxiety turned black and white
to slide out through his finger-ends.
Now, perhaps, he heard only inner voices
singing in breathless phrases,
blurring harmonies so tight he sweated;
smiled only at the dancers leaping on his retina.

Then one August morning there was nothing
but an empty hum,
an unresponding keyboard.
And so, in answer to the daily question, he said
Yes, today I think I will.

Epitaph for George Russell, London

He's gone at last, my ex-belov'd, they've taken him away;
four men in shorts heaved him across the front-door step
and down the mock York stone.
I'd yearned for him once,
enjoyed wild fantasies we'd make each other sing,
pleaded to bring him home.
But I came to hate his seven-octave grin,
his reproachful presence in the dining room.

Poor George. For years he stood and glowered,
ignored except by gifted visitors.
Each day I swore that when my life allowed, I'd make amends.
When the time came I did my best:
whole mornings I reached out to him,
ran fingers up and down in every mode,
strove to master scales, chords and arpeggios,
exercised Czerny till my shoulders froze.

I limped through fugues, stumbled over suites,
picked up, pressed on with waltzes, rondos, preludes, minuets –
usually transposed to keys
with fewer sharps and flats.
I bagatelled and barcaroled,
laboured at scherzo, polonaise, courante.
To no avail: there hardly ever was a truly perfect fourth
and grace notes simply weren't.

On rare good days the notes would syphon into my hands
and arms: a splash of Danube here, a shaft of Moonlight –
first bars only – there,
so at the end of my determined time,
I'd drop the lid, caress its polished curve.
But overnight my fingers leaked
the crochets, quavers, semibreves I'd persevered to learn:
by dawn they'd gone.

So I gave up. Rejected, he resonated blame.
Now he's cast out with all those memories
of lunch-hour lessons in the dining hall,
the heavy tread of RSM Grade IV.
No, George, you weren't at fault.
And those poor men will never guess
your half-ton heft of iron and mahogany weighed less
than guilt.

The search for perfection

I should like to astonish Paris with an apple
                                        Paul Cézanne

Petals brown too fast: he must paint apples
smelling of leaf and bark, air, beaded rain.

Brushstroked in ochre, crimson and vermilion,
smudged by the thumb, here and there's a smear
of white to show the angle of the light.

Bite one: pink under the peel, cool on the teeth,
sweet-acid on the tongue. Crack the nutty bitterness
of pips that won't begin again.

Skins crumple over sunken flesh; the air is drunk
with aging; still he isn't satisfied.

By the time he signed, the only smell was linseed.
Paris sneered.

Comprehension test

There was the clouded eye of the Friday fish, slatted seats
on trains, basins for breakfast drinks, and no flat bread.
The limestone Lycée swallowed us, stored us in cells,
bounced back our laughter down its corridors, sighed
from its drains at Midland vowels.

I looked up to the haughty on a catwalk, down on strollers
in the Bois from a fiacre which cost several thousand francs,
each sou a seedling dibbled from a tray and pressed
into a pot. With heels in holes from unfamiliar shoes,
the Champs Elysées saw me slipper-shod.

I learned to breathe garlic-Gauloise air, and the twist & flick
of table 'foot' from Rob of Loughborough. Tipsy on the scent
of coloured light in Notre Dame, I lost my girl's-school heart
to Alistair who bought me grenadine. Even the crossing
     from Dieppe
couldn't dim my longing to return.

Now there are different mysteries: blind-bend overtaking,
whether to retain the knife and fork, when does *Bonjour*
become *Bonsoir*, the favoured way of administering drugs,
graves like greenhouses, church clocks that double-chime
and how many kisses.

Foot down

How they unwind themselves, these ropes
of roads: from slates to pantiles, apples
to olive oil, war graves to sailors' cliff-top
cemeteries. Tolls hurry us through forests
hung with black kites; mountains fade
into parallel horizons. After Clermont-Ferrand
the rise is marked: five ... seven ... nine hundred metres
plus. In the down-slide, Norman Foster's miracle
stretches over Millau to the Grands Causses
flecked with close-cropped sheep. We squeeze
through blasted rock, hang over rivers, see tarmac
simmering and on the rush taste Fitou, Corbières.
My northern soul starts to unwrap its leaves –
a brussels sprout becoming a gardenia.

The calorific value of anxiety
for Emma

I stalk you through the atlas,
study weather, calculate the time
it must be there, decide you're heartless
then that probably it doesn't seem
an aeon-and-a-half to you, among
the smells, noise, flavours of exotic places;
and when at last the phone *does* ring
I shrug away your reasons or excuses.

Consider all the parents, lovers, partners
fretting for backpackers, peace-
keepers, explorers, migrant workers,
their worry gathering in clouds like gas.
Harnessed, this energy could power
a small country for a year.

Fahrenheit 451

I dream of quires and reams, of foolscap, broadside,
crown, A4, demy and double elephant, drawn by
their lodestone charm. I don't crave dolly-mixture shades
or raspberry or lime. But I can't remain indifferent to
sheets milk-white as arrowroot or pads of pallid cream.

There's the echo of a vegetable past – wood, hemp,
esparto grass, linen, sugar cane, or pulped and
rolled again. The finish pulls my fingertips – rough
handmade, calendered or cartridge, antique or art,
whisper-thin bible, ribbed laid with watermark.

I'm dizzied by its latency, its patient waiting
for my pencil's scratch, a readiness to capture words,
to crowd and crawl them out along its lines.
Paper returns to earth or burns to feathers on the air.
It's history and power.

How to build a cathedral
in memory of Ralph Beyer

First sweep the ruins for unexploded bombs;
sift rubble for what to keep; clear blocks dressed
centuries ago. Now lay roughcast stone on stone
into undercroft, chapels, porch and saw-tooth nave.

Leave gaps. Fill them with angels scratched
on panes or allelujahs of many-coloured glass.
As furnishings: a cross of timbers black with fire;
Christ in glory on a floor-to-vaulting tapestry.

Find a man, a refugee, with skill and flair. Give him
words and tablets set into the zig-zag walls.
In a nave unholy with welders, masons, scaffolders,
watch him sketch, breath curling, on the stone.

Eccentric capitals grow from the chisel's bite,
line on line. He brushes off the dust, tilts his head
to judge the fall of light. No two letters are alike
but amassed, sing rhythmic harmony.

Don't ask his faith or how his mother died
or whether in this place of reconciliation
work is freeing him. Admire the craft, how it
blends into the whole – this covenant.

Quartet for the end of time
by Olivier Messiaen

It seemed that the horsemen
had broken through the seals.

Men scuffed between huts:
snow creaked under clogs
that gnawed their feet;
breath blurred heads,
settled on patched uniforms
wrenched from defeated troops.

When the aurora borealis flushed the Silesian sky,
one Frenchman's faith hardened.
Because there never was enough
black bread or cabbage boiled to rags,
his dreams rang bright as cathedral windows.
He pinned eternity to a stave,
shaped hope in sharps and semiquavers;
shared his vision.
Cracked lips called birdsong from a clarinet;
swollen hands flicked at piano keys
to conjure gongs and trumpets;
fingers barely thawed
stopped strings
as two bows spun prismatic arcs.

Four hundred men
barbed-wired together
fattened on rainbow music.